Our Big Blue Schoolhouse

**A thirteen-year-old boy describes his adventures
sailing down the coast of West Africa**

Matthew Herron

To Oliver who keeps me on the highway— thanks. With Mary Matt Herron

This book is dedicated to my mother, Jeannine Herron, whose compassionate heart and courageous spirit have helped guide me through many of my life's adventures. Without her, this book and the stories it contains, would not be possible. I am both lucky and proud to be her son.

Our Big Blue Schoolhouse
By Matthew Herron

Photographs © 2010 Matt Herron.

Edited by Jeannine Herron
Designed by Marcia Friedman

ISBN 978-1-933945-15-6
Library of Congress Control Number: 2010937615

Talking Fingers Publications
San Rafael, California
www.talkingfingers.com

On a sunny afternoon in July, 1970, I set sail for Africa from New Orleans with my Dad, my Mom and my sister, Melissa.

I was thirteen and Melissa was eleven. My parents got this crazy idea because they thought we were watching too much TV and needed to learn more from real experiences. Well, we had "real experiences" all right! It was quite an adventure, and we were gone (and out of school) for 18 months.

What they had in mind was a very different kind of school. My parents thought my sister and I would learn more from "a big blue schoolhouse" than we were learning in our traditional "little red schoolhouse" at home, and I guess we did!

Our boat was a 31 foot sloop, with a single mast and mainsail, and jib. Below (inside) there were two bunks for me and Melissa in

We discovered a game we could play on the foredeck. When the bow of Aquarius rose up on a wave, we would leap into the air. Then the bow would fall below us, and we would be flying.

the forepeak (the front part of the boat), and berths for my folks on each side of the main cabin. There was a head (a toilet) and a galley (the kitchen) with a stove that was gimbaled (on rockers so it would be level when the boat heeled over). The rest of the space was mostly lockers for the food and clothes and tools and about a hundred books that we brought along.

To reach Africa we sailed east from New Orleans along the gulf coasts of Mississippi, Alabama, and Florida and across Florida by canal. We made a nine day passage to Bermuda, and then sailed for 26 days across the Atlantic to the Azores. We stayed in the Azores almost two months—we really liked it there! Eventually, we made a seven day run to the Canaries, stayed there another month, and then made the last eight day passage to the coast of Africa.

We all kept a log (like a diary) to write about the things that happened and what it was like to cross the ocean in a small boat. My father, being a photojournalist, planned to sell picture stories from Africa to help pay for the voyage.

This book is from my log about our adventures as we made our way down the coast of West Africa all the way to Ghana, visiting Mauretania, Senegal, Gambia, Sierra Leone, Liberia, and Ivory Coast along the way. (The two Guineas were pretty much at war, so we skipped them).

It starts as we are leaving Mauretania…

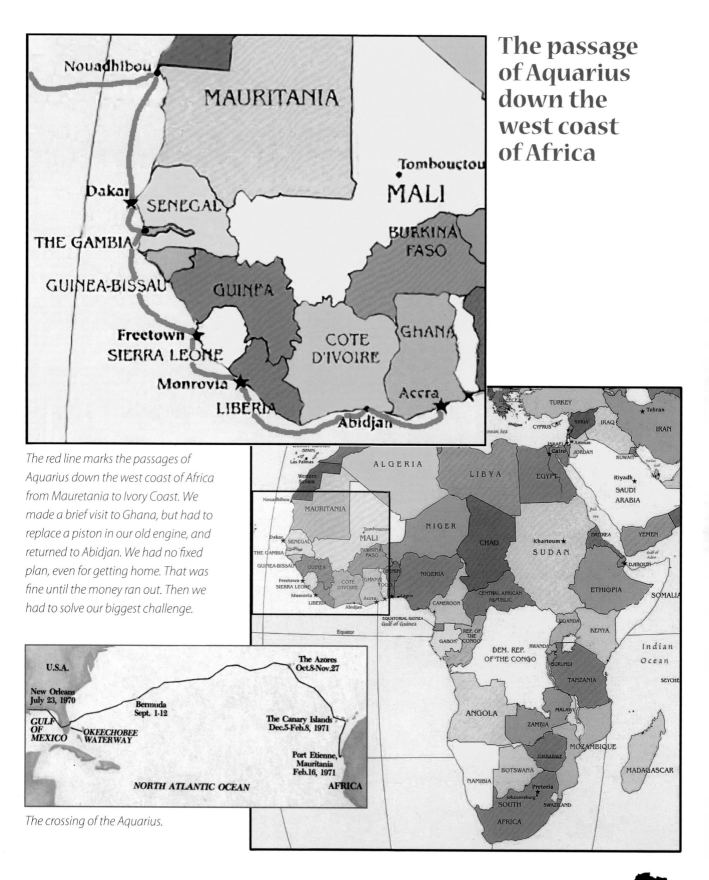

The passage of Aquarius down the west coast of Africa

The red line marks the passages of Aquarius down the west coast of Africa from Mauretania to Ivory Coast. We made a brief visit to Ghana, but had to replace a piston in our old engine, and returned to Abidjan. We had no fixed plan, even for getting home. That was fine until the money ran out. Then we had to solve our biggest challenge.

The crossing of the Aquarius.

Leaving Mauretania To Sail To Senegal
Port Etienne (Nouadhibou)

Saturday, February 20, 1971

WE WERE WALKING DOWN THE DOCK when some Ghanaian fishermen came over to sing and see us off. Their boat had been detained at Port Etienne (which is now called Nouadibou) for three months because they were caught fishing in Mauretanian waters. Mom got her guitar and we all went to sit on the dock and listen. The music was very nice, almost like American rock. When the singing was over, we cast our lines off and set sail for Dakar. The wind was from behind and the tide was going full force with us so we were making a good six knots. We set the vane and for the rest of the day we just read and slept in the sun.

Sunday, February 21

SINCE THE VANE GEAR wasn't steering a very good course, Dad decided to put up the twin staysails. They can be attached to the tiller (steering handle) when we are sailing before the wind and they will steer the boat themselves (at least in theory). Getting the sails up wasn't so hard, but making the boat steer a good course was. Dad tried lots of different things and after four hours he finally hit a combination that worked very well. For the rest of the trip to Dakar no one touched the tiller. It was steering great.

My dad navigated using a sextant, and we built a "chip log" (a piece of wood in a rope harness) to cast behind the boat to calculate our speed. As the "chip log" floated away behind the boat, we counted the knots in the rope for ten seconds as it passed through our hands. That's how many "knots" we were going.

Once a land bird flew onto the boat, too exhausted to fly. We fed it some tuna and finally it flew away.

Monday, February 22

This day was a big one. We started it out with our first day of school since the Canary Islands. We listened to the news and looked up Israel and Egypt in our world Atlas. We had a biology lesson in reproduction. I asked for a handwriting lesson. My handwriting is very poor because I am left handed. We also wrote in the log. We had not been very good about that. As a reward for doing school we treated ourselves to a piece of chocolate. After school I made a fitting for the bottom step of the companionway that I could use as a typing table which I needed very much.

Birdman strikes the water again! Able to swing around tall sailboats with a single rope! Fighting for truth, justice, and his own way!

In the evening Mom decided she was going to make a cake. Out came the collapsible oven and cook books. She picked a (yum yum) chocolate cake with (yum yum yum) chocolate icing. In about an hour she and Melissa had the batter in the oven cooking. Our oven doesn't work very well because when you put it on the stove, the burner is under only one side. This made one cake cook faster than the other.

When the cakes were almost done, Dad shouted "Dolphins!" We all came running out and sure enough there they were. We hadn't seen any in a long time. Anyway this was a very large school. There were maybe 50 or 60 of them but they were small. They darted through the water just under the bow. One of them actually hit the boat with its dorsal fin. For some reason the water was not as crystal clear as it had been around the islands or out in the middle of the Atlantic ocean. Still, you could see ten or twenty at a time. Suddenly I saw something fantastic. As a large swell passed us a dolphin leapt out of the water and as his tail came down he flopped it over and made a loud "crack!" Then they were all doing it! Doing half somersaults in the water.

After a while I went inside to see how the cakes were doing. They were out of the oven and Mom was taking one out of the pan. She got it out in three pieces and also found it was burnt on the bottom.

Melissa made the icing which was supposed to sit for twenty minutes, but after half an hour it was still very soft and gooey. I decided to go to bed. In another half hour Melissa came in and announced that we were going to have runny icing on our cake. It was runny but it was good. One cake disappeared in about 15 seconds.

After the cake I went back to bed again only to be awakened at midnight by Melissa yelling with joy. I went out on deck to see what was happening. The dolphins were back! This was something special—the phosphorescence in the water made them glow! They looked like comets streaking through the water leaving long glowing tails behind them. The air was very cold and I only had short sleeves on so soon I went to bed again.

There were lots of things to do on the boat to keep from getting bored. I made "baggy wrinkle" (frazzled rope to protect the sails if they bumped against the stays), and macramé, and woven belts. I even read books—something I hardly ever did at home.

Tuesday, February 23

HAVE YOU EVER HEARD OF ALFALFA SPROUTS? They are delicious. I grow them on the boat and they are our daily fresh greens when we are at sea. The seeds are very small and brown To grow them you need five large mayonnaise jars. That is all. Fill one of the jars with one inch of water and stir in two teaspoons of alfalfa seeds. Soak these overnight. On the second day, pour the water out of the first jar. Fill the next jar with one inch of water and put the seeds in it as you did before. Rinse out jar #1 and start some more seeds in it. On the third day, move the seeds in jar #2 to jar #3 and keep rinsing and moving the seeds each day for five days. When the first seeds have been growing five days they are ready to put in your salad. You must always

keep your plants in darkness as they will think they are underground. Just put them in a box with a lid on it.

We did school again. This time it didn't last so long. We studied the digestive system and after that we somehow managed to slip away from writing in the log. Day after day it was steadily getting hotter and hotter. I got myself a pillow and slept in the sun for a couple of hours.

Finally I started getting too hot so I had to find something else to do. I decided to make gigly twirls. My definition of a gigly twirl is anything attached to a string that spins in the wind. First I made a small pin wheel. That worked very well. I hoisted it up the flag halyard. Then I made a paper helicopter. I found that if I held it close to my face while it was spinning, the light reflected off the sides of it would almost hypnotize me. I put three or four of those up for tell-tales (on a sailboat, tell-tales tell you which way the wind is blowing). When it was just getting dark Dad said it was time to take the twin staysails down and change course for Dakar. That was done by eight o'clock and once more we were heeled over. My bunk was (sob) on the (sob,sob) high side (sob, sob, sob!). I had to rig a canvas sling to keep from rolling out.

Wednesday, February 24

DAD WOKE ME UP AT 6:30 for my morning watch. He said I would be the first to sight land. Before he went to bed he showed me how to take the reef out of the mainsail. With full sail up we began to really move. Then he left me with the vane gear to fiddle around with and went to bed. After five or ten minutes of fiddling I got the vane steering a good course so I went below to do some alfalfa farming. Since some jars were

Here is Aquarius "dressed" with all the flags we made for the countries we would visit. The baggy wrinkle I made is on the stays to keep the sails from fraying. Melissa has our folding bicycle.

Mauretania

Senegal

Gambia

Sierra Leone

Liberia

Ivory Coast

Ghana

smaller than others I had to keep transferring the sprouts each day so they would have enough room to grow. I rinsed them with fresh water and poured it off so they wouldn't get moldy.

I kept looking around with the binoculars every so often to see if I could see land. No, after three hours on watch I still didn't see land so I called Melissa for her watch. Boy, she didn't like that. She said "I always have to take watches!", etc, etc. Then Dad came out and calmly said, "Oh, I see land!" In another hour or so Mom said, "There are breakers ahead of us!" She was right! Dad took another look at the chart and discovered that we weren't exactly where we thought we were.

Well, we made a wide circle around those huge waves and headed straight for the harbor. We passed Goree island with some old forts on it where they used to keep slaves before bringing them to America. We raised the Senegalese flag (I made the flag and Mom sewed on the yellow star) and the yellow "Q" flag (for quarantine) to show that we wished to enter the country and to be cleared by the health authorities. We tied up at a large wharf and Mom and Dad went to see the customs and immigration officers.

Russian fishermen bringing us a gift of red snapper.

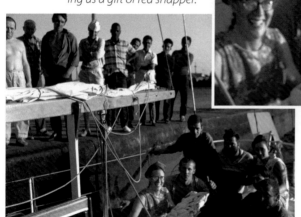

In about an hour they came back. Then we started taking onlookers aboard. One man off a Russian fishing trawler said that he wanted to bring us some fish. He was gone a long time and we were waiting for him so we could move the boat because we didn't particularly want to be crushed at midnight by some freighter coming in to dock. Then the Russian came back. He and another man were carrying a 3' x 1' x 1' block of frozen red snapper! We were very glad we had waited.

Letters Exchanged with a Class in Rochester, New York

Dear Mr. Herron

I read with interest the New York Times story about your plans to sail to Africa. As a teacher, it is easy for me to see how much your children will learn from a trip such as this—a real learning-by-doing project.

Now I have an idea, you may or may not be interested in for Matthew. The newspaper said you would be doing several writing assignments while on your trip. Well, I have an assignment for Matthew (for which I am willing to pay)—one letter a month to my Social Studies class (10 and 11 year olds) telling about life aboard Aquarius and a little about ports of call along your route. My class will follow your trip on a large map and learn through Matthew about people around the world. Does a dollar a letter sound like a fair fee?

If this projects is of interest to you and Matthew, please let me know and I'll send the money the day I receive your letter.

Have a nice trip,
Pat Burke

Questions sent by students in Miss Burke's class:

1. *Do you have a stove?*
   Yes. It's not an ordinary stove. It's "gimbaled" (stays level when the boat rolls).

2. *Do you fish from the boat?*
   Yes. We mostly catch dolphin. That's a kind of fish (dorado) not Flipper.

3. *Do you stop and sleep at night?*
   At sea, Aquarius keeps sailing 24 hours a day, so it's important for someone to always be on watch, looking for ships and tending the boat. Melissa likes to stay up late and I like to get up early, so she takes the watch from 9pm to midnight. Mom and Dad split the next six hours and then I get up at 6am for my watch. During the day, someone is always on deck so we don't keep any regular watches.

   We always wear safety harnesses at night, which are tied to the boat. This is to keep us from falling overboard. (If someone fell overboard while everyone was sleeping it would be the end of them).

4. *Do you sleep on beds or sleeping bags?*
    Both. When it's cold we put the bags on the beds.

5. *Were you scared being at sea?*
    Mom and Dad told us to keep watch for other ships at night because we didn't want to be in a collision with a freighter that didn't see us. Melissa was scared about this, and drew a picture of Aquarius being hit by a big "Bully" with all of us jumping off into the sea. We have seen the lights of ships sometimes in the night, and sometimes it seems like we are on a collision course with them. Freighters carry two masthead lights and the one in front is lower than the one in back. So it's pretty easy to tell if they are going to hit you. If the two lights are lined up, watch out! If your eyes are ten feet from the water line, then you can see about four miles to the horizon. If a freighter is going about 15 miles an hour and its lights become visible at the horizon, it will only take about 16 minutes for it to get to you. That doesn't give you very much time to take action.

This is Melissa's drawing of a freighter colliding with Aquarius. Although such a collision was unlikely, we kept watch at night to keep track of other lights at sea.

Mostly the ships are on one side of us. The best way to tell how they are moving is to line up the ship's lights with something on our boat—maybe the mast, or a stay—and watch it carefully. If the lights move, you're ok. But if they stay in the same position, you need to take evasive action! Dad told us that if that happened, we were supposed to wake him up. Then he would check out the situation and change course if he thought we should. You never know whether a ship will actually see you, even though we have a radar reflector fairly high up on a stay. In the middle of the night, the officer on the bridge of the ship might not be paying very close attention—in fact he might be asleep at the wheel!

6. *Do you ever get seasick?*
    Not really. Just queasy sometimes. My mom does though.

7. *Do you get any storms and have to stop?*
    Yes, we get storms just like anywhere. When we are at sea we just have to keep going. We "reef" the sails to make them very small. We had some gales at sea and very big waves!

8. *Did you have to learn Morse Code?*

   A little. And here's a message for you to decode!

Morse Code Alphabet

A	.−	J	.---	S	...	0	-----
B	−...	K	−.−	T	−	1	.----
C	−.−.	L	.−..	U	..−	2	..---
D	−..	M	−−	V	...−	3	...--
E	.	N	−.	W	.−−	4	....-
F	..−.	O	---	X	−..−	5	.....
G	--.	P	.--.	Y	−.−−	6	−....
H	....	Q	--.−	Z	--..	7	--...
I	..	R	.−.			8	---..
						9	----.

Full stop .−.−.−

Comma −−..−−

Query ..−−..

Message

..../..

−.−−/--- /..− / /.../..../---/..−/.−../−../
/−.−/−./---/.−−//

.−/ −//.−.././.−/.../−//−/..../.−./././
/.−.././−/−/././.−./...

../ −.//−−/---/.−./..././/−.−./---/−.././
/−/---//−.−./.−/.−../.−..

..−./ ---/.−.//..../././.−../.−−/.−.−.−

.../---/... .../---/... .../---/...

S O S means "SAVE OUR SHIP" (dit dit dit dah dah dah dit dit dit). Or you can say "diddy dit dah dah dah diddydit" Anyone who hears it, anywhere in the world, will know you need help!

---

9. *Do you have a washing machine?*

   No. We don't have room for such luxuries. We save up all our dirty clothes during a trip and wash them when we get to land.

10. *Who washes the dishes?*

    We take turns. The person who gets the dinner lets the others decide between them who gets the job (excluding the cook).

11. *Do you have a bathroom?*

    Yes. It's called a "head". It's just a toilet inside the boat. In the olden days, sailors used to go to the head of the boat to use a seat that hung over the side.

12. *Do you have electricity?*

    Yes. We have two 12 volt car batteries. We don't use electricity much. When the engine is running it charges the batteries. We also have kerosene lamps.

13. How much water does your water tank hold?

It holds 75 gallons. That's about as much as some houses use in a couple of days. We use it mostly for drinking. We can wash and even cook with part sea water.

14. Do you have running water?

No. We have to pump it out of the tank. There are two pumps in the galley sink. One pumps fresh water from the tanks and the other pumps up sea water for washing dishes.

15. Did your mother and father take you out of school because they felt you needed to know something about the outside world? Or was it just a pleasure trip?

We didn't like our schools in New Orleans. My folks thought we would learn more on the trip. This way we're having fun too.

16. Don't you get bored?

Sometimes we do. But there's lots to do and we make friends in the places where we stay a while. There are usually kids who speak English to play with.

17. Does it cost a lot to take a trip like that?

The boat cost $6000. I don't know how much we spent getting ready and stocking the boat. When we got to Africa, after about two months in Dakar we learned all the prices and how to bargain. You would be surprised how cheaply we live. With all costs included, like boat repairs, gifts and taxis and food, we spend about $75 a week.

18. Did you have to learn how to make a lot of knots?

Yes. It was fun. The most important one is a bowline and here is how you make it. You should practice it because you will use it a lot in your life. It's not just for boats.

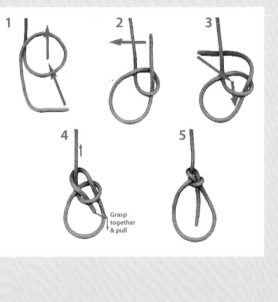

Imagine the rope at the number 1 as a "tree".
1. Loop the tree rope around to make a "rabbit hole" beside the tree. 2. Imagine the end of that rope as a "rabbit". Make the "rabbit" pop up through the hole and go around the "tree". 3. Make the "rabbit" go back down into his hole. 4. Pull tight and you have… 5. A bowline

Exploring Dakar, Senegal

Thursday, February 25

WE WENT INTO DAKAR to have a look around. We went to the American Embassy for mail and Mom and Dad talked to the consul. They wanted to find out some things about Senegal. Then we went out in the streets and looked around for a place to eat. We were getting very hungry when we found a snack bar.

All the boys on the street were trying to sell us something. They called us "toubabs", which means something like "foreigner" but it's not an insult. Mostly they wanted to shine our shoes. One boy came up and asked Mom if he could shine her shoes. We all had sneakers on! He didn't seem to care. Mom pointed to her shoes and the boy took that as a consent. He knelt down in front of her and started taking out some white polish. Mom said "non!" but he didn't seem to hear. The next thing we knew he was brushing white polish on Mom's sneakers. She repeated (in his ear) "non! non! non!" He got the message and backed up. A few minutes later we saw him working on another victim. There he was kneeling down putting white shoe polish on this poor man's sneakers. The man was getting very red in the face. He kept shaking his finger and saying "non!" Finally an African told the boy to leave. But all through our lunch we were being offered magazines, gum and cigarettes. It was very annoying. We spent the rest of the day looking around Dakar and saying "no!"

The markets were always full of people and fascinating things. We loved to look at the amber and trade beads and ju-ju's (amulets to ward off evil).

Friday, March 13

WE GOT UP EARLY to catch the "car-rapide" into Dakar. It is the size of a VW bus and is always full of fifteen people and babies with a few extra hanging on the back and baskets of fish on top. We were going to the marketplace to do some shopping.

We went into a huge circular dome that looked like the top of a temple. It was just crammed with tables and booths. Everywhere people were hurrying around. First we went to a meat stand which was just an ordinary counter with corpses hanging all around—sheep, rabbits and chunks of beef. Hatchets were flying down and bones were splitting. Crack! Crack! Crack! Mom was

What would it feel like to be able to roll your eyes in any direction? Very bizarre!

learning how to bargain from a friend. She bought some lamb and some huge shrimp (one was half a foot long!)

People were always trying to sell us parrots. They would perch all over their owners and squawk at us. Around the outside of the market was a path and on either side of this path there were stands with every fruit and vegetable that you could imagine. We got apples, oranges, potatoes, carrots, lettuce, parsley—all with loud bargaining and women tugging Mom this way and that.

We were interrupted by five or six boys running madly through the crowded path. Running after them was an old old man with a very very worn stick. He was screaming at them. A minute later I saw them tearing back, knocking over people and plants. The man finally caught one of them and while hitting

Sometimes we got to watch a healing ceremony or tribal celebration.

him with the stick, led him into the market. Our friend, Mrs. King said that the boys were not supposed to be in the market and if they were caught they might be put in jail.

The last thing we bought was strawberries. They were big and luscious and cost about thirty five cents for a kilo! We put those carefully on top of the pack, praying that they would survive the bus trip back to the boat. We snacked on a kind of peanut brittle—peanuts, or "groundnuts" as they are called here, are the main crop of Senegal so you can buy roasted peanuts for a few pennies (francs) on every corner—while we looked for a place to eat lunch. We found a Lebanese restaurant and had Shwarma sandwiches. Mmmmm!

The Island Of N'gor
(near Dakar, Senegal)

Monday, March 16

THE AMERICAN AMBASSADOR invited us to live in his beach shelter on N'gor and we stayed there several weeks. We were finding so many interesting things along the beach and in the tide pools that Mom had the idea of making an aquarium. We filled a dinghy with sea water and put sand and shells and seaweed in it. Sea slugs were plentiful—they just washed up on the beach. We had all sorts and sizes. They "flew" through the water by undulating like a ray. We watched them eat, defecate, copulate and lay eggs.

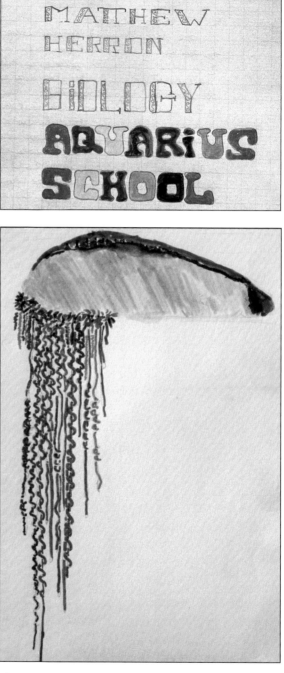

The creatures we brought to our dinghy pool were good for hours of entertainment. It was fun drawing them, too.

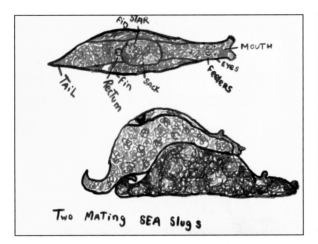

Two Mating SEA Slugs

SEA SLUG CRAWLING

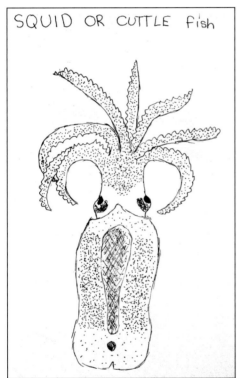

SQUID OR CUTTLE fish

Top left: Melissa's drawing of two sea slugs mating. There were always long strings of eggs in our dinghy pool; Top right: My drawing of a crawling sea slug; Bottom left: The cuttlefish (drawn by by Melissa) is like a squid but it has a cuttlebone inside that helps it go up and down in the water. Sometimes people put one in parakeet cages to give their birds calcium. They can change color very fast.

Tuesday, March 17

ONE DAY I FOUND A SEA SLUG washed up on the beach. Its head was like a snail's only with two extra feelers in the very front. This creature did not have any shell at all. It was all soft on the outside. In the middle of the body there were fins similar to a sting ray's The sea slug uses them to to swim through the water very slowly. They also move like a snail over the sand. When the slug is crawling, the fins fold up to protect a very soft sack on the back. There is a tube coming out of this sack that I think is the anus. Right before the feelers on the top of the head are the eyes. They are just very very tiny black spots on the skin.

The only defense I can see is its camouflage—black and white like the sand. So far I have found that the sea slug eats seaweed. It seems to have a mouth under its head. By its sack are what I think are the gills, and on the sack is a silver star. Right under the sack, inside the slug are all the organs.

Once I found a sea slug that had a long cord coming from its anus. I couldn't figure out what it was. It was a pinkish color with spots on it. The spots were eggs. Later I discovered that some eggs were laid by the slugs in our aquarium. The sea slugs, when frightened, shoot out a purple liquid that clouds the water like an octopus. This must be another form of defense.

In our book, I found out that the sea slug is really called a sea hare and that the feelers on its head are really smelling organs. The sea hare belongs to the mollusk family. It will contract into a tight ball if you mess with it. The sea hare has both male and female sex organs and I have seen four slugs mating each other.

Wednesday, March 18

ONE DAY I WAS DIGGING A VERY LARGE PIT in the sand just for fun. All of a sudden the sand on one side of the pit started moving. A crab stuck his head out and then quickly backed

into his hole. He started shoveling sand into the mouth of the hole so I wouldn't see him. I, however, had seen him and I started going after him by digging a larger hole with a bucket. Soon I caught him. He was very strange. His body was square and very thick. He was pale yellow with bits of red here and there. His eyes were very strange. First of all, if you looked into them and moved your head, they had the same effect as a three dimensional post card. Secondly the eyes were very long. They looked like a contac capsule. The third and strangest thing about him was that he could move his eyes out of their sockets to an upright position so he could see better.

Ghost crabs roam the beaches mostly at night and in the day they sleep in underground burrows to keep cool. They can run very fast and they pack a good pinch. The crab I had seemed to be right-handed because he always raised his right eye first; his right pincer was biggest; and when he ran sideways he ran to the right.

A GHOST CRAB

EYES

EYES FOLD
DOWN INTO
HERE

MOUTH

I suppose they are called "ghost crabs" because at night they look like little ghostly shapes scuttling across the sand. At night they are safer from birds and other creatures who want to eat them.

As part of our "biology class" we studied the creatures we found, and tried to find out everything we could about them from observing and drawing them.

We also collected sea urchins, starfish, anemones, jellyfish and anything else we could find. Mom even found a man-of-war (a very poisonous jellyfish). It was very large with a pink balloon and long purple tentacles. We made a cut in his balloon to see if he could repair it. He just shriveled a little around the cut and stayed full of air. The balloon was very tough. After we removed him from the aquarium we found two dead fish with his tentacles on them.

The only trouble with the aquarium was that we had to dump the water out twice every day and put fresh in. It took a long time to fill that aquarium, but it was pretty and we enjoyed watching all the activity that went on in it.

When we had written down everything we observed, we looked them up in our books to see what we had missed.

This sea urchin is sticking to my fingers with the suckers it uses to stick to the rocks.

Thursday, March 19

THE WHOLE FAMILY went out on the rocks to look for things for the aquarium. I found a pool with small fish in it and I put my bucket in a narrow passage in the pool and scared the fish into it. I caught two fish that way. We found another larger pool with fish but they hid under rocks. Dad got the great idea of draining the pool. We got the fish we wanted and then filled it up again.

There were beds of sea urchins. They were snuggled into weird depressions in the rocks—hundreds of them. We had to watch our feet. If you get a spine in your foot it can get badly infected.

Tuesday, March 24

WE WERE GOING TO HAVE A PARTY with our African friends. They were mostly seventeen and eighteen year old boys who ran the pirogues (canoes) between the mainland and the island of N'Gor where we had the boat anchored. They were going to bring their guitars and make African music because Mom wanted to learn some.

Pape, (pronounced "Pop") one of the boys who had kind of adopted us, took Mom to his compound in the village where his sisters were preparing Senegalese food for the party. They came back in the pirogues with great flowered bowls of rice and sauces.

We got started with the music right away. They liked American music too, especially James Brown, and another friend Carter who was from a three-masted schooner played rock for them. Dad got out the tape recorder.

Pretty soon Pape came out with two big plates of something that looked like fortune cookies. You were supposed to put some red sauce on them and I found out too late that it was like eating fire. The trick, I learned, was just to keep eating and eating and then you don't know your mouth is in ashes until the end. My mouth burned all night. About five songs later I snuck in and took some of the main course because I was starving. It was rice and meat with sauce. Mom tried not to give me too much fire-sauce.

By the end of the evening two high strings off the guitars had been broken. I went into my pup-tent to sleep before the party was over but I had a hard time because Pape kept pulling the front stakes out and making the tent collapse. Finally he quit and I got to sleep.

Bottom photo: We loved the markets. This guy is spinning some cotton thread for weaving while he waits for customers.

Expedition From N'gor To Shop In Dakar

Friday, March 27

WE GOT UP AND TOOK AN EARLY PIROGUE into the village. Mom had brought along a bag of caramels to give to the children in the village while we waited for the car-rapide. Melissa lit the fuse by giving three children some candy. Pretty soon we heard the ground start to rumble. I saw a huge cloud of dust come around a corner. It started to head straight for us. All the time shouts were coming from the inside of it.

It kept growing as it got nearer to us. Suddenly we were all blinded by the dust. The noise doubled in volume. The first thing I saw when the dust started to settle were arms and hands and legs and feet all waving in every direction. I saw Mom holding a half-empty bag of candy up in the air frantically trying to pass it out fairly. Then an old woman came over and grabbed the bag. She didn't get it away from Mom but she had a good grip on it. She was pulling on it like her life depended on it. Finally all the candy was gone. The children stood around and showed us how much candy they had gotten until the car-rapide came.

In Dakar we went to shop for African material. We went into a shop where the walls of its two rooms were just filled with every kind of material imaginable. There were about twenty tailors at little tables which spilled out onto the sidewalk, all busy sewing.

After that we went through the spice market. There were bags and tables of strange roots and crystals—some looked like sap from trees. The smell was indescribably wonderful! Outside I saw beads, rings, silver, necklaces, gold, jewelry and all kinds of ju-ju's (good luck charms) in one glance.

When we were nearly there we stopped to photograph an ant hill that was solid as a rock and taller than me. It was in the shape of a man. We could see three or four in one field.

Monkey See, Monkey Destroy
Bathurst (now known as Banjul), The Gambia

Monday, May 31

THERE IS A SMALL GAME RESERVE in Abuko about 15 miles from Bathurst, the capital of Gambia. We had been introduced to the man who ran it so we decided to take a trip out there. On the way we stopped to pick up Elizabeth, a new friend of Melissa's. She was the only one who knew the way to the reserve. Her parents said that we would see lots of birds and monkeys and maybe some other animals.

We turned into a road at Elizabeth's directions and found ourselves in lush jungle. This was strange because we had just come out of a landscape with not much vegetation at all. Dad talked to some people and they led us through a gate. Just then Eddie Brewer, the director of the reserve came along. He said just follow the path and nothing could happen. He also told us that we might meet his daughter, Heather, on the trail taking some young chimps for a walk. "They are friendly but rough" he said. "The main thing is not to be afraid of them. If they come at you, just make a noise like a panting dog. That means 'I want to be your friend!'"

We started out on the sandy path. It seemed to me that Tarzan was going to swing down from the next tree. Birds were everywhere. We walked a long way down a winding path. Elizabeth, Melissa and I went ahead to explore. All of a sudden I froze in my tracks. Way up high in a tree there was something moving. It was coming down! I turned around to tell the girls but they were already running full speed the other way. I went after them. Melissa dragged Mom and Dad along to the spot.

Close behind them came Heather. She had a chimp in each arm and one holding onto her skirt. Another one was just running away with a filter from one of Dad's cameras. Finally Heather came back with an empty filter case and Dad went off into the bush to find the filter. It took a while, but it was finally discovered—in a chimp's mouth! They were everywhere at once, but very friendly as Eddie had said. They didn't try to bite very hard.

We stayed in that spot and played with them for about an hour. Their favorite game was to use us as trees. They also had a bad habit of pickpocketing anything that was shiny. I had a pair of binoculars around my neck and one chimp just insisted that he wanted them. When he couldn't have it that way he started to unscrew the lenses. Suddenly the strap broke and he went crashing to the ground. Next he started on my shoelaces. One hand for each shoe.

Five or six screaming chimps came at us. From trees, from the ground, from vines, from everywhere!

The chimps were frantically excited and curious. They wanted to see everything we had with us. They examined things mostly with their mouths by lipping to determine the texture and feel. Mom got some unexpected kisses!

That one chimp was always chasing me around. We had to be very careful about walking under trees too. A chimp was bound to swing down on our heads. Heather, after getting the roughnecks out of our hair, walked with us along the path. With all the noise the chimps were making we didn't get to see any other wild life.

An hour later we came to a clearing that had a few large cages in it and a small rest area. There were two antelopes running around loose. I petted them while Heather gave the chimps some mangoes and apples and put them in a big fenced-in area which was built like a playground only better. When the chimps are older they will live in the wild. Heather takes them out every day to get used to it.

After repairing the binocular strap, we moved on without the chimps. Mom and Dad stopped and waited quietly for about ten minutes to see if they could see any animals but we went on. They did see some Red Colobus monkeys. We heard a monkey but he didn't show himself. I saw what I thought might be a snake trail so we ran quickly over that part of the path.

When we came again full circle to the beginning of the trail, Elizabeth ran straight to the water tap and washed her hair, face, shoes, legs, hands, arms and half her dress (by mistake). Soon we were on our way, half starved, and still thinking about those little devils with four arms!

Yamendow N'jie (left), queen of tie dye, and her friend, gathering the stamped cloth to make the tightly tied bundles that will go into the dye vat.

African cloth

Wednesday, June 2

WE WENT TO VISIT YAMENDOW N'JIE, a Gambian woman who does African tie dyeing and batik printing. We wanted to see the whole process and buy some of the beautiful cloth.

We came into her compound and found Yamendow sitting outside on a bamboo mat, tying up long pieces of cloth. First she folded the material in half lengthwise. Then she held part of the crease she had just made and pleated the material like a paper fan with her other hand. This would make designs of bulls-eye type circles. Next she would take a piece of string from a young boy who was just untangling a big mess of it and tie the fan of cloth in several places. She would put about three of these designs in a piece of material one yard wide and six yards long. (This is just the right size for a "lapa" or African skirt).

After she had done this to several pieces of cloth, she laid another piece on the mat and started to gather it in with both hands, sprinkling once in a while with a bit of water. It looked like she was clawing at it. Soon it was all crumpled up in a little circle. She then wrapped a piece of string all around the cloth bundle and pulled it tight. It looked like a pancake wrapped in string. That was all we saw the first day.

We loved Yamendow's cloth so much we wanted to make our own.

Yamendow is setting the dye in her special brew.

The second day she was making batik prints. She had a little fire going in a grill with a big dish pan of old candle wax on it. Some boys from the compound were setting a table with one leg up on a barrel for the printing of the cloth. Yamendow took one of the wooden stamps that she uses and dipped it in the wax. She stamped the cloth with it—the pattern looked like a tree with leaves. She did the whole cloth like this in repeated patterns. I was trying to figure out how she was going to get that permanent looking black wax out of the material. She picked up another stamp shaped like a half circle and made some wavy patterns with it, giving the stamp a good shake before pressing it on the cloth. Yard after yard she printed on the undyed material. Then she crumpled it like she had the day before, only she didn't pleat the circles into it. Her husband came out with a parrot and put it on Melissa's shoulder. It climbed down the back of her dress with its beak and claws.

The next day we watched Yamendow take the cloth out of some indigo dye (made from the indigo plant). She transferred it to a boiling barrel of water with her "special medicine" in it. We never got her to tell us what the medicine was made of. I think it was made of some sort of leaf but I'm not sure. This process got the wax out of the cloth and set the dye more permanently. Then she washed the cloth in cold water and hung it up to dry. We bought three lovely pieces.

Mom asked Yamendow if she would teach us how to do it. Yamendow said yes and agreed we could have our own stamp made with the "AQUARIUS" symbol on it, the same design that's on our flag. So we gave her a drawing and she had her carpenter make us a stamp. We were planning to make thirty yards so there would be some to give away as gifts.

Our Big Blue Schoolhouse

When we arrived to make our own material, first we had to wait for the wax to heat up and boil. Yamendow put a great big pot on an outside wood burner and then went away to do something else. Soon she was back and ready to go. It was tricky learning how to stamp a solid clear design without dripping wax on the material, but we learned fast and we all took a turn with several pieces of different colored cloth. Then I bunched up my cloth and tied it and she did the rest because it was getting later.

The next day Yamendow was making brown dye out of kola nuts. (Africans love kola nuts and it is a mark of hospitality to offer kola to guests, but they are very bitter and I can't imagine liking them.) First she split the nuts in half (we helped her), then they were put into a sort of wooden bucket that is used for chopping or grinding different things. Two women pounded away at it with stout sticks in rhythm until the kola was just very small chunks. We tried pounding too, but Yamendow got impatient with our slowness. They put the pounded kola into some water where it turned a rich brown color.

Soon the dye was ready to go on the cloth. Yamendow picked up a handful of pounded kola nut from the bottom of the dye and squeezed it over the flat pancakes of cloth. Then she sprinkled the juice over it too. She did this to all the pieces of cloth, then carefully put them in a basket and covered them with plastic so the sun wouldn't get to them.

Our next visit found Yamendow at a large barrel with a fire blazing under it. She was doing some more cloth with her "special medicine" and she was starting to do ours too. It was all purple from the indigo dye it had just been in, but it came out of the barrel absolutely beautiful.

We made a stamp of our Aquarius logo, then dipped the stamp in wax and stamped it on the cloth.

The kola nut dye has to be boiled and stirred.

We are trying our hand at pounding kola nuts for dye, but the African women think we are pretty slow.

I couldn't believe we had made it ourselves. Later that afternoon when everything was dry we took it home and tried to think of things to do with it. I wanted to make an African suit.

A few days later we discovered that a friend had a sewing machine so we took it off her hands for a few hours. Mom and Melissa made skirts and a dress. Also four pillow cases for Aquarius. Everything looked great. Then we remembered that our stamp was still with Yamendow—she might make more material with it and then our cloth wouldn't be original. Well, you can't have your stamp and keep it too!

Hanging our cloth up to dry, we're feeling very proud.

I'm gathering my cloth together for tie dying.

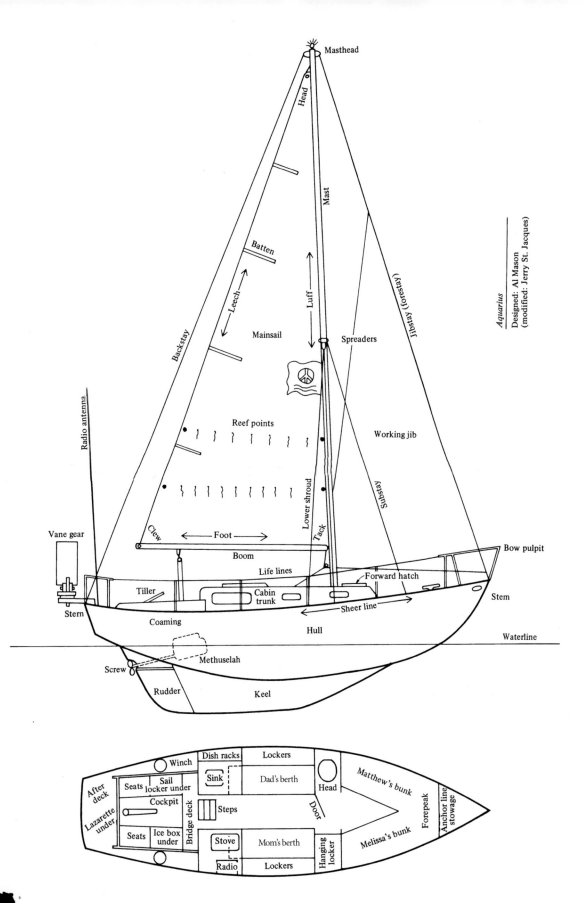

Masthead

Head

Mast

Batten

Jibstay (forestay)

Leech

Luff

Backstay

Mainsail

Spreaders

Aquarius
Designed: Al Mason
(modified: Jerry St. Jacques)

Working jib

Reef points

Radio antenna

Substay

Lower shroud

Vane gear

Clew

Foot

Tack

Bow pulpit

Boom

Life lines

Forward hatch

Tiller

Cabin trunk

Stem

Stern

Coaming

Sheer line

Hull

Waterline

Screw

Methuselah

Rudder

Keel

After deck

Winch

Dish racks

Lockers

Lazarette under

Seats

Sail locker under

Sink

Dad's berth

Head

Matthew's bunk

Cockpit

Bridge deck

Steps

Door

Forepeak

Anchor line stowage

Seats

Ice box under

Stove

Mom's berth

Melissa's bunk

Radio

Lockers

Hanging locker

There's always a lot of work to do to keep the boat in shape and get ready for long passages.

Our Big Blue Schoolhouse

How the "Afro" Got to Africa

HAIRSTYLES IN AFRICA are not what Americans think they are. I asked a Gambian woman where the 'Afro' hairstyle came from, and she said, "From America, of course."

The hairstyles we have seen here are elaborate and involve lots and lots of braids. Sometimes the hairstyles are named after important people or events. The big fashion right now seems to be the "General Gowan"—a spiral of braids with a big fountain-like top-knot. I guess a Nigerian general named "Gowan" came to visit here.

Sometime ribbons or strings are braided in. We began to ask the names—there was the "Snake", the "Boy's Part" and the "Straight." The girls sit for hours to braid their hair—friends do friends, sisters do sisters. The hair-do's last about a week and then before doing the whole thing again, they can wear a "nafo", the traditional African headdress.

Top left: the "General Gowan"

Bottom left: girls doing hair

Top middle: the "Johda"

Bottom middle: another view of the "General Gowan"

Top Right: traditional Africa headdress, the "nofa"

Into The Interior!
200 Miles Up The Gambia River

Sunday, June 27

I woke up to hear the engine running and people running around up on deck. We were finally leaving Bathurst after a month of being stranded because we were waiting for one little engine part to be shipped to us. Dad went off to get some ice while Mom went shoppping. Melissa and I stayed behind to clean up the very messy boat and get everything ready to go.

It was Sunday so almost all the stores were closed. Dad went all over town for ice with no luck and Mom couldn't find any alcohol to light the stove with so we had to use lighter fluid.

We finally got off the dock and headed for St. James Island. Aquarius sailed for two or three hours and then we anchored at the island. We had lunch and then took a little nap. I stayed up and worked on a hammock that I intended to sleep in that night. Just then the American Embassy's launch appeared on the horizon. It was coming in our direction very fast. In about two minutes I could see Mr. and Mrs. Kepferle with their two daughters and two boys from Liberia. The boys were American but had lived in Liberia for six years. Jack, the youngest was twelve and Wasill was fifteen. I discovered from visiting them in Bathurst that all they do all day is play Crazy Eights! All day! Sometimes they would go outside but not very often.

The motor launch took us to the island and Dad and Mom rowed in with the dinghy. The island was very small and getting smaller every year. The whole thing was eroding. James Island used to be a fort. In fact it used to be many forts. European soldiers fought over it because anyone having a fort on the island could control the whole Gambia River. People thought there was a lot of gold in the Gambia, and also the white men came to

There were forts all along the coast where goods were traded and slaves were brought to be put on boats and taken to America.

buy slaves. There was only one problem. Health. The water was contaminated and the food was contaminated. The people in the fort had to fight malaria and many other diseases. One time seventy one men died in three months. So many different countries wanted that little island that the fort was destroyed and rebuilt about ten times. I could see old rusty cannons from the first fort and newer ones from later forts side by side. All there was left were crumbled walls and towers.

Along the shores we found pieces of glass because one general liked to drink brandy and there were tons of old pieces of glass. There were also beads. They were used for trading, something like money. A few of us found pieces of pottery. Even teeth from goats or other livestock.

Monday, June 28

THAT DAY CONSISTED of just motoring up river and doing a bit of sailing. We anchored just below Kau-ur. (map on page 42)

Tuesday, June 29

WE SAILED ALL DAY until we got to Kau-ur and there we stopped to meet the peace corps people. It was late evening so we went up river and anchored again.

Top left: Sunset over the river; Top right: In Gambia the women seemed to do a lot of the work; Bottom right: A Gambian girl and her sister.

Wednesday, June 30

THAT DAY THINGS STARTED TO HAPPEN! Dad got up and got the boat under way. All the time the waters were getting calmer and calmer. The river was strange to me because I always expected a river to flow down stream but this one went both ways with the tide. So sometimes we were zooming along and other times we were barely moving. In about the middle of the afternoon Mom spotted a creek branching off to one side. We all got into our small dinghy and started to row up.

The stream was about 20 feet across and both sides were covered with thick foliage. The sky was overcast luckily for us because otherwise we would have fried. There were many birds. Huge eagles flew ahead of us landing a little farther up stream. Small swifts darted about. They looked like bats. Once Mom saw something that was as big as a bird but its wings seemed to be transparent and a shade of bright yellow. It fluttered across the river and into a tree and we never saw it again.

Soon the bugs started to come. Most of them were flies but there were some tsetse flies which are three times as big as a regular fly and can give you sleeping sickness with their very painful bite. The others I could not begin to identify. Luckily we had brought some bug repellent with us and everybody except dad put some on. They were still very annoying. They didn't land but were content with buzzing around my ears. I really hate that. It almost drives me mad.

As we sailed up the river, we visited some villages along the way. When you come to a village, the custom is to seek out the chief and let him get to know you a bit before going into his village. We gave this chief and his relative some kola nuts and a photo of the boat as a souvenir. Kola nuts have a bitter taste and contain caffeine. They are much prized among Africans.

We always saw and heard neat things when we explored small streams in our dinghy. The bird calls were all wonderfully different from anything we heard at home. There were flocks of weaver birds that swarmed together like schools of fish and wove strange nests that hung from trees.

The reflections on the water were the best. All along the bank palm tree leaves had fallen half way into the water. The reflections made beautiful gods-eyes patterns. And the symmetry was beautiful also.

Farther and farther we went up that creek and narrower and narrower it got. In some places the bugs would go away completely. All at once Mom spotted a big reptile. It was about a foot long and might have been an iguana. Or if it's head hadn't been shaped like a snake, an alligator. But I think it was just a very very large lizard.

We moved on. All different kinds of birds were flying around. Dad was very busy trying to get it all in with his camera while the rest of us just watched. I had a line out the back of the dinghy and we were dragging it along the bottom very slowly. We didn't catch a single fish in the whole river Gambia. Not that we tried very much but we still didn't catch anything. Not even a boot! About an hour and a half later Mom decided to turn back because we would be getting mosquitoes soon and they would come thick as rain.

While rowing back a very long two miles I managed to break a rotten oar. Water had gotten in where some screw had been and rotted it out. The corners in that little creek seemed to be endless. Every time we went around a bend, I thought that we would come out in the river. Finally I started recognizing this plant or that tree and before I knew it we were out on the river.

After we all had cleaned up the wreckage of getting ready to go, the Aquarius was headed up river. In the evening Kuntaur was sighted and it was there we spent the night. Kuntaur is a large village with one store that sells gasoline. There is a general market in the middle of town and maybe one canned goods store. It has a ferry to get people and rice across the river. There was a rice threshing machine until it got sent to Bathurst for repairs. When it is gone the women just pound the rice in big wooden bowls. Just about all that anybody eats is rice and something else like fish or some sauce, sometimes just plain rice.

Anyway we spent the night in this village tied to a ferry. THERE WERE TONS OF BUGS AT NIGHT! They came about dusk and we just got the screens up in time. Some were very small. In Florida they call them No-see-ems. They go through screens and the smallest little crack. The worst part is that they BITE! There were also things that looked like baby dragon flies. I THINK that they were harmless. We lived through it and the next time, we put the screens up earlier.

Thursday, July 1

LATE IN THE MORNING we were off again. About an hour later we were coming to a fork in the river. It was made by an island. All of a sudden a pirogue came up to us and told us to go one direction while our map told us to go another direction. The two men in the pirogue said that the Lady Wright, a river steamer, went that way so we tried it. We turned and gathered speed but were hindered in our forward motion by the fact that we had just run aground. (This was the first time since Florida when we also got bad advice).

We were very badly aground. Our water line had lowered two or four inches and it was high water. The engine was useless. An anchor was put out at our stern but it wasn't put out far enough so when Dad used the winch to try and pull us out the stern was pulled downwards. This made a little groove in the bottom of the river where our keel rested.

The men in the pirogue went out to get the anchor out but failed so Dad went out with them when they came back and he failed too. For the next half hour there was a lot of talk with no results and finally dad got out our anchor and put it into the very tippy pirogue with three men in it. When the men in the pirogue had rowed him way across the river he dropped it in the water. He came back and tried pulling us off using the winch again but it only resulted in slightly damaging the winch so it slipped all the time. We were all very discouraged by now. There were only a few more tricks left to try. The groove the keel was in made things very difficult.

The next line of attack was to make the boat draw less by tipping it over on its side. I untied the jib halyard and swung out over the water and the boat tipped slightly. The boom was swung out and the jib halyard was tied to it to hold the boom up. Melissa and I walked out on this rig and then some fishermen in another pirogue came and held on to the dangling end of the jib halyard. The knot used in tying the boom up was just one half hitch so if the man in the pirogue let go we would all go tumbling into the water. I told him not to let go but he misunderstood me and thought I meant the opposite. There was a mad scramble for the rope. The knot was slipping! Then it happened. All at once I caught the rope!

The boom was put out on the other side and we hung out on it again. The boat tipped over and we cranked the winch again. We were slowly moving! To top the day off it started to rain a little bit. At last a half hour later the boat was off the mud. The men in the pirogues said we didn't go far enough to the left when we rounded the island point. This time we ignored them and went back the way we came and then at a fork took a different and surer route. As we left the men in the pirogues were still waving frantically for us to go in the other direction. We made the passage around the islands all right with no more incidents.

Towards evening we started seeing monkeys. When the mosquitoes started to come we anchored by a tribe of baboons. It was late so they didn't go away but were content with screeching and shaking the trees. Soon it was dark and the monkeys settled down to sleep. I did the same. It had been a very eventful day but only the beginning of fun and adventures.

Now…the real thing and heeeeer it issss.

Friday, July 2

I WAS AWAKENED by the soggy heat. It was late in the morning and mom and dad had already eaten. Soon after Melissa got up, with her usual growls and grumbles. When I looked outside almost all the baboons had left and the rest were hurrying away as fast as they could. Mom and Dad however had gotten up before the monkeys and taped them waking up and being enraged at seeing the boat still there. They took it out on the poor palm trees. Shaking them with all their might and then tearing leaves off and throwing them on the ground. It was all there, right on a little piece of brown magnetic ribbon.

Just when I had finished listening to that fantastic tape, I heard mom say "Now all we need to see is a hippo!" No sooner said than done! A hippo surfaced on the other side of the river with a loud snort. The next second it was gone. All this time I had the misfortune to be down below with my sister so I didn't get to see him.

When the boat was cleaned, Dad up-anchored and the Aquarius was on her way up river under power towards Georgetown. Georgetown was a very British town and very isolated from everywhere. We met some peace corps people in a shop and they had been trying to get into Bathurst for a long long time. The only trouble was that there were no taxis or buses or anything. After some discussion over whether it was safe for us to go any further without a guide, we left without the guide and our stomachs filled with cold coke. One setback of the river trip was that we couldn't get ice in Bathhurst so we had no fresh meat. We were motoring along very fast because the tide was with us.

Suddenly the boat lurched upwards with ear splitting scraping sounds. This greatly distressed me. It sounded almost like we had gone on the rocks. By poking my head out the hatch I discovered that the bow was one or two feet higher out of the water than it should be. So the Aquarius had finally gone on the rocks—her first time! The two-knot tide was pushing us up against the rocks making it impossible to move. Melissa and I tried rowing out to drop an anchor but the tide was too strong.

So we waited. We fished, getting the lures caught on a rock almost every cast. After about an hour the tide changed and began to rise and we were able to get off. From that point on we were very careful about our navigation. Towards evening we docked at the village of Bansang. Almost the first person we met was Mark, the peace corps volunteer there. He had been staying in the village for one year. He had built his own house African style, out of mud bricks and a beautiful grass roof. Mark spoke the native language which was Wolof and everyone in the small village knew him by name. That night there were a lot of bugs but we got the screens up in time and slept very well.

Mark's house.

Saturday, July 3

WE INVITED MARK up the river with us since we were only going about forty miles further. Dad coached him on steering the boat and he took the helm for most of the time. On our way up in the morning Mom spotted a boa or a python near the water. It was about ten feet long and didn't seem to care about us at all. We did circles and passed by it several times but Melissa was the only one who didn't get a good look at it. Our anchorage that night was by flocks of birds all singing their different tunes. It was very peaceful.

Sunday, July 4

IN THE MORNING we went on a little further to a creek. In the dinghy we tried to go up it but the tide was too strong. Before we drifted out however, everyone saw a green water snake swimming across the creek just in front of us. Soon he was out of sight behind the trees and we started back down the river.

Bansang was reached about noon and we all climbed up a hill to where the wireless station was, to have a look at the surrounding country. I soon discovered that by putting my ear to the wire supporting the radio antenna and tapping it, I could reproduce something like the soundtrack of a space movie. It sounded like ray guns or lasers depending on whether I hit the wire with a key or the palm of my hand. Soon everyone had their ear to the wire and I was banging away with key and fist.

Mark pointed out to us a native celebration called a "simba" in which one man dresses as a leopard and goes around and chases all the children of the village. When he caught one he must pay a forfeit or dance in front of the crowd. We went down to watch and take pictures but unfortunately we were all caught and had to dance.

Mark invited us for chop (food) at his house and we all said we would come. The dinner was cous cous which is something like rice, meat and that special peanut sauce. It tastes something like peanut butter mixed in with plain gravy and meat. There was only a little bit of sand. Now it just so happened that that day was the fourth of July and it also just so happened that we were Americans and it also just so happened that we had an extra Spanish parachute flare.

So that evening Dad sent up a flare with the villagers cheering and everyone watching. All the little children ran away in fright. Some people said that there were some hippos just around the corner of the river that came out in the morning so that is where we spent the night. I tried sleeping outside but there were too many bugs. No hippos were sighted.

Here we are docking at Bansang. The whole village came out to see us because no boat like ours had ever been there before.

Our Big Blue Schoolhouse

Monday, July 5

WE LEFT BANSANG early in the morning to go back down the river. We took along Mark and a friend of his in the peace corps to help us get water at the hospital. We took a tour of the hospital with the doctor, got our water from him and left. The wind was against us so we motored. Our anchorage that night was where we had slept with the baboons before. They were still there.

Tuesday, July 6

WE SAW LOTS OF WOMEN working in the rice fields. They are very strong. It looks like the women do all the hard work in Africa while the men sit under trees and talk. Well, not always—we did see a man climbing a palm tree with a collecting gourd to tap the sap for palm wine.

There was wind against us so we motored. In the afternoon we sighted hippos! They were cruising around by the banks. Dad got his cameras out and we went over there. They didn't seem too afraid of us. They just kept moving away and we kept following. The only problem was that when they moved, they moved under water so we had to guess where they were going to come up. Sometimes one would surface ten yards away and be so surprised to see us that he would dive under immediately and come up very very far away. After about an hour we lost them so we went away.

A stilt-walker in a village ceremony.

About half an hour later we got one of those storms called "tornados." We could see it coming on very fast. The black clouds were like a wall advancing on us. When they were overhead the wind came. It was incredible how fast it all came on. And then way up the river I saw an almost solid wall of water coming on very fast. The waves were already beginning to come. Luckily we had got the anchor down just before the wind came. If we hadn't, we would have been blown on to the shore because you can't make an anchor hold when the boat is pitching around and being blown away.

Mom and Dad decided to take a fresh water bath. That was a mistake. When that rain hit I heard Mom scream. The rain was coming down so hard it was stinging her. Dad was running around tying everything down outside and Melissa and I were watching it all from inside.

We loved the strange trees in Africa. This is a banyan tree.

By now the water was being whipped off the waves. Our poor dinghy was being blown around like a toy balloon on a string. Every once and a while a big gust of wind would come and up would go the dinghy spinning and tipping over and smashing into the vane gear. The storm lasted only about twenty minutes but it was a good one.

Mom made some delicious chop suey after the storm was all over. We spent the night at Kau-ur anchored under the trees.

Wednesday, July 7

I WOKE UP in the shade of the trees. Everyone else was up except Melissa who was shortly when she heard something about breakfast. Dad and I were in the process of moving the boat over to the Kau-ur dock when the engine cut out and I couldn't get it started again. Luckily we had just enough momentum to make it to the dock against a tide. It was discovered sadly that the gas tank had a leak. We were also out of water. A very kind man on the dock gave us some water from his personal rain water supply. He showed us where to get gasoline and get the tank welded. We waited the whole day doing this and we didn't get off until five. Then we had a short swim and anchored just after Elephant Island.

On July 8 we had strong winds against us. In the morning we passed James Island and in the late afternoon we got back into Bathurst. We ate at a restaurant that night to celebrate.

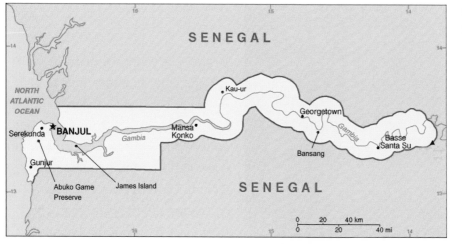

Map of our journey through Gambia

Net Making and the "Dash"

Bathurst (now known as Banjul), Gambia

Thursday, July 15

ALL ALONG THE AFRICAN COAST, we saw people fishing with nets. I watched how they cast their nets and I tried casting one myself. It's not easy! To cast a net, you hold it with your hands and teeth. There are two important things to remember when you throw it: Open your mouth (or you might lose your teeth), and be sure to hang on to the end of the string.

So, I was finally getting a casting net made. My old one was too big and heavy for me to throw and it was also made out of cotton string that would rot. In Bathurst there was a net maker called "the pa" by everyone, even me. This man was very old with round cheeks and bony hands. Almost all his teeth were rotten but he always wore a smile.

One day my fisherman friend Salieu took me to see this man about a net. When we came into his compound he was seated on a very low stool making a net at the fantastic speed of two loops a second. His shuttle was long and thin. He kept it wet to make the knots tighter.

Salieu talked to the pa in very fast Wolof. He acted as my translator and in that way I found out that the net would cost one pound ten shillings, or seven dalasies twenty bututs, or three dollars sixty cents. I

went right down to the store and got six shillings worth of the right netting twine. I brought it to the pa with some heavier string to go around the bottom of the net. I gave him one dalasi to buy the lead weights and then I came home to the boat.

The day after the next, Salieu and I went to check on the pa and found that he had not done very much. This was due to the fact that the whole project depended entirely on his gods. So we went away and came back in the evening of the next day. We found it all done except for the bottom string and the leads for the bottom of the net. The pa said the man who makes the leads didn't make them on time and that they would be finished and on the net by the next evening. The next evening I was back again and the net was finished.

I paid the pa and then the ritual of "dashing" began. I dashed the pa the remaining string from the net and he dashed me a shuttle full of the string to repair my net with. Salieu dashed me an empty shuttle. The pa wanted it so I dashed it to him and he dashed me another shuttle full of string. I dashed the pa the leftover heavy string and I dashed Salieu the leftover lead weights. I also dashed Salieu my old net because he didn't have one and he had helped me a lot in learning how to throw and make nets. He dashed me a piece of bamboo to make a mesh stick the width of my net and I dashed him some gum for his kids. Before we left I dashed Salieu a box of matches that he had used to seal the ends of some ropes for me and some money for his newborn baby girl (named after my mother). My last dash was a new customer for the pa, a friend who also wanted a net like mine. And so the mad dasher slowly sailed into the setting sun.

More questions from Miss Burke's class
Questions about Africa

1. *Do they have food markets in the places where you stop?*
   Yes. They have to, or how would the towns-people get their food? They are mostly open air markets where farmers bring their crops.

2. *Do you see elephants and giraffes?*
   No. West Africa doesn't have big game like the African animals you see on TV. Those are mostly in the south and east. The biggest animals we have seen are hippos. We came face to face with baboons when we were on the Gambia River and hippos too, and they are very wild, but there is a large gap of water between us and I don't worry too much.

Top left: We always had to find the nearest market when we came to a new place. Melissa was our ambassador she would find ways to communicate with people and make friends wherever we went. She always found the market first; Middle: Some kind of lizard; Bottom left: This wild cat is called a serval cat. Although it's not very big, it can jump up to 16 feet in the air to catch a bird.

3. What does Africa look like?

The scenery in Africa varies from snowy mountains to deserts where it is boiling hot and monotonous as a blank sheet of paper. In most places the countryside is full of green fields of grass with lots of palm trees and a few baobab trees. The coastline is just miles and miles of beautiful beaches dotted with an occasional village. Lately the temperature at high noon is about 90 to 100 degrees. I've gotten used to the heat however and I don't mind it too much.

4. Do Africans have pets?

The most common pet is a parrot or a canary. I met some Germans who had driven across the Sahara Desert in a VW bug. In their car was a hawk, and something I have never seen before. This animal had scales with yellow spikes on the ends of them. The head was pink and the tail was shaped like a file with a flat side and a curved one, but he could curl it up. He had a very long tongue. It was an anteater! Later I saw a bush baby at someone's house. He was a little furry ball that bit. He walked like a sloth. His eyes were very big for seeing in the night and he made small noises like a monkey.

Melissa and a bush baby.

5. Do you speak African?

I had plenty of trouble talking to people in Africa at first, but now I can talk pidgin English and a little bit of French, Spanish, and Portuguese. I can't talk any African languages except a few words of Wolof, but people say it is very easy to learn.

Greetings from Rochester
My students are enjoying this project. You are doing a great job of helping other kids learn about the world through you.
Good Sailing,
Miss Burke

Thief In The Night

Freetown, Sierra Leone

Wednesday, August 25

WE HAD A LOT OF TROUBLE with thieves in Freetown. We were robbed (they say "t'iefed" here) twice at about three o'clock in the morning by men boarding the boat while we were sleeping.

(I must tell you here that Mom bought thirty boxes of "Angel's Delight" a dessert we discovered in the Canary Islands but had never found again until Freetown, so she stocked up.)

One night in the middle of the night my bunk felt like an erupting volcano. There were tremendous shouts and yells and it seemed to me that the boat was lurching terribly. I jumped out of bed and into a lot of confusion. Dad was yelling "Get the gun!" and Mom was digging under the bunk for it. Melissa was screaming but soon stopped. When Dad had the gun he fired one shot into the air. By now I realized that we had been t'iefed and the t'ief had been caught in the act. Dad was just trying to give them a scare. The gun went off with a loud "CRACK".

A motor launch came out with some police on it. Dad gave them a light and they went off to look for the thieves. There were three. Mom told me that one had come down the companionway into the cabin and had his hands on the bag of Angel's Delight when Dad leaped out of bed and scared the daylights out of him. Dad grabbed hold of the bag of Angels Delight as the man fled and it ripped, saving our wonderful dessert! But the intruder jumped into a waiting canoe and got away. Wouldn't it have been funny if he had gotten home and found his loot to be thirty boxes of Angel's Delight?

I walked up to the foredeck to look for the launch. I just happened to glance down the hatch when Melissa started screaming. The more she screamed the more she shrank into a ball away from the hatch. Then Mom ran into the forepeak from the cabin and flung a pillow up at the hatch, shouting "hey!" I called out, "It's only me" and things calmed down a little, except for Melissa. She was furious with me. How was I to know she couldn't see my face from inside? The rest of the night she slept with Mom and Dad and the next night she slept all huddled up in the very fore of the forepeak. The night after that she slept with the hatch closed so we all nearly suffocated. If I would just say "BOO!" to her she would hit the ceiling and go into a fit of rage.

You won't believe what that one shot did to the city of Freetown. The next morning NINE detectives and inspectors came with photographic equipment and a fingerprint kit to investigate (not the thieving, the SHOT). They came out to the boat and filled up the cockpit. They perched on the after rail and on the cabin-top. It would have been impossible to get them inside! Unfortunately Dad was away looking up old sailing accounts of the exploration of Sierra Leone so he missed the fun.

After Mom had dictated a statement to one of the men he told some of their side of the story. When the shot was heard they got the President of Sierra Leone out of bed at three o'clock in the morning and moved him to another place. Everyone was alert for an attempted coup. (There have been two such attempts here recently). Evidently the shot was heard for miles. Some people even said there were six shots. One of the detectives took our gun to headquarters for inspection but they brought it back the next day. In a few days we left Freetown WITH OUR ANGEL'S DELIGHT, over the bounding main!

Cooking at sea

IF YOU THINK COOKING IS HARD, try doing it this way. All the pots and pans and things I set down migrate from one side of the counter to the other with the roll of the boat. There is beef jerky hanging from the grab rails waving above my head. If I try to beat an egg, I have to chase the bowl all over the galley. And then sometimes I start feeling queasy and have to quit and let it burn, or I will just finish cooking a wonderful meal and then feel too seasick to eat it. It almost takes an acrobat to jump around and catch all the dishes that are escaping. It is the best training I know for fast reflexes.

We found kids to play with along the way and learned about what they liked and what they did for fun.

Onward to the Ivory Coast
Fish Town, Liberia

Wednesday, October 20

It took us seven days to get from Monrovia in Liberia to Abidjan in the Ivory Coast. A friend we met in Monrovia came with us because he loves to sail and he got off at Harper at Cape Palmas. We anchored for a few days off a little island in a small bay near a town called Fish Town.

We were swimming and playing along the beach of the island and began to find beads in the sand. They were the kind of beads that Europeans used for trade more than two hundred years ago. We got excited and really looked for them, and found a lot! Later we heard that the island had been a burial island and that these beads had probably been left with the folks who were buried there long ago, and eventually washed down to the beach and the sea.

We did some diving in the rocks and reefs, and Dad and Mom found African lobsters that gave them mighty undersea battles. But they made a yummy dinner!

The local kids were very curious about us and brought us fresh coconuts. They let us try out their dugout canoes. We had great races and surfed with the waves. A bit tippy, but fun!

We could find almost anything in the markets in Bouake. These bowls are made from a type of squash.

Hammerhead Shark!

Friday, October 22

THE REST OF THE TRIP to Abidjan was slow. NO wind. We came upon a strange tidal event. It looked like two currents had come together and stopped. The area was full of flotsam (and jetsam, whatever that is) in a long line as far as we could see. And just below the surface the sea was teeming with life. We saw huge jellyfish pulsing along, and then suddenly a big shape! It was coming closer! It was the weirdest thing I have ever seen. It was a hammerhead shark with a head that looked like he had bashed headlong into a wall at 500 miles an hour. I decided I wasn't going for a swim right then.

Coming into Abidjan

IT WAS EXCITING coming in to the harbor at Abidjan. There is a very narrow entrance and the wreck of a large ship outside the entrance to show you where you shouldn't go. The huge harbor inside flows in and out of that narrow entrance with every tide and we had to wait a bit for an inflowing tide before trying to enter. It took quite a while to get down the channel and it was almost dark when we entered the harbor. The lights of the city in the distance across the harbor were beautiful (and confusing). It's hard to find the navigation lights and judge distances. We were all helping Dad by counting the blinks on the buoys.

Abidjan was a bustling, modern city with a big port. We decided to take a train "upcountry" to Bouake to visit the interior. Every time the train stopped, women came up to the windows with everything imaginable on their heads!

Upcountry by Train

Wednesday, October 27

JUST AS THE TRAIN BLEW ITS WHIS-
TLE, we scrambled aboard into the second
to last car with our tickets and found
ourselves in the luggage section with some
other people. There were benches along
the wall, but they were full so we sat on
our packs. The train started up, gained
speed and we were zooming past grass
and villages. Hurray! My first train trip!
In Africa!! There was only one set of tracks
going through the countryside, and the
grass and weeds were growing so close
that I could have touched them. In fact
I did with my shoe.

We started to slow down and we were stopped
next to a very small station of a very small village.
Villagers came to the train carrying plastic bottles,
dolls, and imitation wicker jugs. It just so happened that we had forgotten to take water with
us, so we decided to get some at the next station
because the train was already moving.

The country was already changing. There were
gently rolling hills of banana trees on either side
of us and once in a while I could see a rice field

*Top right: Waiting for the train to start on our trip to Bouake.
It's fun to get off the boat and see more of the countryside;
Bottom right: This is the only way to get to the smaller towns.
These taxis carry everything from chickens to firewood.
And people squeeze in wherever there is a space; Bottom
left: Women were the heart of the markets. Most of them
had children on their laps or on their backs or playing nearby.*

I liked to watch the people around the train. The children always seemed to be very happy.

in one of the low spots. The sky was blue and cloudless. The next station was just a dirt path with a house to one side. We looked for people selling water bottles, but there were just women and girls walking with huge bowls on their heads. Some were selling hard boiled eggs. That's all, nothing else. Just hard boiled eggs. People were leaning out the windows of the train and bickering for them. The train moved on. We were getting kind of thirsty.

I was sitting on the top step in an open exit when we went into some kind of cut through a hill. It was deeper than the train and the walls of it were dirt going straight up very very close to the train. It went on for a couple of miles and it was very dark.

The other people in the baggage section had boxes and baskets and the usual big enamel bowls. One lady had five or six empty bowls. The train was stopping again and this time I saw that the women were selling coconuts and cabbages. The lady with the bowls kept buying cabbages and cabbages until she had at least thirty five.

We bought some coconuts. The lady chopped off the tops of them and the inside was full to the brim with juice that was fizzy and not at all like the coconut milk I am used to. It had a coconut flavor but it was clear. That took care of our thirst, but the coconut meat was very rubbery and I didn't have any. Some people were buying thin sticks of wood that Africans use for toothbrushes. The whistle blew and we were off again flying through the grass at seventy miles an hour. The day got hotter and the country got more jungley until I was expecting to meet Tarzan.

In about an hour the train stopped again and a few people got on and off. Here they were selling cabbages and some sort of fried meat with sauce, and oranges. That crazy lady bought thirty more cabbages! I couldn't figure out what she was going to do with them. Her bowls and boxes were over flowing and there she was sticking her head out the window and bargaining for more. All the cabbage ladies at the station were crowded around her thrusting cabbages under her nose. And she was still buying more!

I Love Sailing

Thursday, October 28

Ever since I sailed our seven foot Styrofoam Sea Snark in New Orleans, I have been in love with sailing dinghies. In New Orleans, I had a boat that looked more like a bathtub. I made the sail myself and it was in constant need of repair. But it sailed. I used to sail around the maze of canals in the New Orleans yacht club even though most of the time there was no wind. Once I even rented a sunfish for an hour and that really got me hooked. There was a stiff breeze and Melissa was constantly screaming in my ear, "Matthew!! Don't tip it over!!"

My sailing tub was made of fiberglass, but it wasn't well finished and every time I got into it, the glass worked its way into my skin and stayed there for a long time. ITCH! ITCH!

It was not until we reached Dakar in Senegal, that I got to sail by myself again. We were staying at a beach house on an island and right in the front yard were two Sunfish. The owner hardly used them and once he took me out for a five minutes, but I just sat in the middle of the boat because he said if he came forward the boat would nose under.

We moved our boat to the yacht club harbor and there I met a man who owned a small catamaran. He told me again and again that he would take me out and nothing ever happened. Finally he promised he would the next day. He left his sails up all night and in the morning he found that they had rubbed against the stays and torn. So I never got my sail. I could have strangled him.

Then, in Gambia, the assistant director of the Peace Corps let me sail his boat. I sailed it with a boy called Merrill, who I also saw later in Monrovia Liberia. It was fun, but the tide was very strong and we had to watch it.

In Liberia I took two trips to a place called Sugar Beach. It was a fresh water lagoon about a mile long. One of Merrill's friends, Todd, brought a mini sail and we had great fun. It was very very tippy. The second time we came, we spent the night, but it rained.

The last and best place was Abidjan, Ivory Coast. There was a huge lagoon inland and we were anchored off a French yacht club. It was a natural harbor. Abidjan is a big city so the yacht club was big. Also, the French like to sail. They had five classes of boats. Small ones for the children were "Optimistes". Then there were two sizes of "Ponos". Then "Red Balls" which had a huge sail area and too many ropes to handle it. Last were the cruising boats including two trimarans that were built in Ivory Coast. They had many races and I was in two of them—the first we

This is my watercolor of a race in Senegal

came in about tenth and the second we came in third. I got to sail the Optimistes every Sunday.

So when I get back to the states I am going to get a sail boat I can race, or if I can't have that maybe I will turn to soaring or BOTH! That's better still.

Stranded In Africa?

Friday, October 29

Mom and Dad have been talking a lot about how to get home. We thought we would just sail back to New Orleans, but they've been figuring everything out and it would take maybe 40 to 50 days to cross the Atlantic from here. And we are running out of money. (The magazines my father used to shoot photos for have gone out of business). And actually we will be going to California because that's where Mom is going to finish her Ph.D. So how would we get the boat to California? This is a BIG PROBLEM!

Mom asked a shipping company how much it would cost to ship the boat back on a freighter. About $5500! That's almost what Dad paid for the boat in the first place. And that would just be to New York. Then what?

Some friends from the French Yacht Club came to look at the boat today. We've decided to sell it and fly home. Sob!

Wednesday, November 3

Our friends didn't want to buy the boat. When they heard our story they decided to try to help us because they work for a shipping company. They sent the dimensions and weight of the boat to the Maersk Lines to ask about shipping it to San Francisco, and the telexed reply estimated $562! Wow! They think maybe it was a mistake so they have asked for another estimate.

Hitch-Hiking Home

Friday, November 5

The estimate was correct! Hurray! Aquarius will go to San Francisco! And our friends are also asking a British company whether we could return to the U.S. on one of their ships. Dad has offered to exchange photographs for our passage, because he has photographed for *Life* and *Look* magazines, and is a good photographer.

Saturday, November 6

The captain of an Elder Dempster freighter has telexed that he could take one passenger, but not a family because the only space he has is the pilot's cabin. Our friends say we should meet him when he arrives and explain that our boat is probably smaller than the pilot's cabin! We would probably fit in one of their lifeboats! Maybe he will let us go with him.

It is a British training ship for marine cadets. There would be lots of things for Dad to photograph about how the boys are trained. Maybe I could teach them about how to cook at sea! We have our fingers crossed! This would be the best solution!

Monday, November 15

It's settled! We met the very nice captain and he says if we don't mind the pilot's cabin, it's OK. And I can sleep with the cadets if I want. We will only have to pay for our food.

We had our second Christmas on the boat before we left Africa. We made a "tree" out of paper" and hung our stockings from the grab rail. Even though we didn't have a chimney, Santa came anyway!

Leaving Africa

Now that it looks like we're really leaving Africa, I'm thinking a lot about what comes next. When I get back to the states, I am looking forward to a lot of things, the first of which is unlimited potato chips. I can eat potato chips until the salt crusts on my lips. The second thing I am looking forward to is being able to find just about anything I want. In Abidjan I couldn't even buy a small spool of wire. The only store that had it, sold it in one hundred yard spools.

I am not looking forward to going to school, but if I must, I will look forward to going to a good school. The last one I went to, in New Orleans, was run like a prison. It even looked like a prison with four guard towers on the corners. Some schools have barbed wire fences around the playgrounds.

When we get to the states, if ever, Melissa wants to get a farm in the country and raise horses all her life. I'm a little more difficult. I want to live by the water so we can have our boat there and I want to live in the country close to the mountains so I can sail plane and I want to live near a big city so I can get all the things I need to keep me happy and I DON'T want to take care of chickens and horses every day! If we lived in a place like this I would be very happy.

The last thing I can think of is just seeing how the states have changed in two years—for the better I hope. There are only a few things I can think of that I am not looking forward to and the first is hearing the questions and telling the same stories about the voyage over and over again 34,267,819 times. Also air pollution, and smog, and trash and slime. But that's all I can think of.

Some of the things I will miss are coconut milk, baboons, and hippos, and sailing in Abidjan. Also, the friends I have made, bargaining, and trips into the country. I will miss Africa, but most of all I will miss being a sailor. When I get a house, I will not consider myself as one, unless I have a boat.

I will not miss malaria, force nine gales at sea, the same old flat, wet horizon, the African markets and taking watches. One thing I will definitely not miss is getting on and off the boat. It's a lot harder than it sounds. Once in the Azores, Dad was rowing out to Aquarius where it was tied up to some lighters. There was a gale blowing and Dad had to row furiously to keep a straight course. When he was halfway out the wind picked up the rubber boat and threw it into the air with Dad in it. Of course, he got a little wet, what with the rain and falling into the drink. But that was all right. He just towed the dingy to shore and everything that was in it with him.

Other times we have waded through slimy slipways and walked on sea moss-covered railroad tracks, a couple of times doing a flip! Sometimes we have to land on a beach in waves and the whole dinghy gets swamped. No. I won't miss that. And I won't miss doing the dishes in a 12 by 16 inch sink and having to pump the water by hand either.

Maybe in three or four years we will get a bigger boat with more room and go through the French canals or something and I will know what to expect and it will be ten times even better than the first trip!

Back to the States

Dad arranged to have a "cradle" built for Aquarius to keep her secure on the deck of the Maersk freighter all the way to California. That's where we're headed, to the area near San Francisco where Mom grew up. She has a job and will finish her research there. We'll live in Palo Alto and go to good schools, and Dad will put together a book about out trip. This amazing adventure is coming to an end.

The Onitsha

The Onitsha is the Elder Dempster Line training ship that took us to New York. Dad traded photographs for our passage. We had a good time on the ship. The captain and the crew took good care of us, and the food was great. I got to know some of the cadets and bunked with them. They were pretty good at ping pong.

Top & inset: The ride back to New York on the Onitsha. We had to practice emergency drills with the cadets. This involved grabbing a lifejacket and putting it on FAST!; Bottom: Trying to fly a kite from the bridge of the Onitsha. It was hard to get it started but eventually it flew.

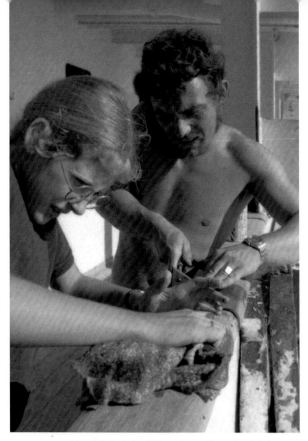

Top left & right: Life on board involved doing school, eating, and helping with chores. Melissa enjoyed swabbing the decks and polishing brass with the cadets; Bottom right: Our bodies thought we were still in Africa. We were FREEZING on the docks and had to wrap ourselves in blankets to keep warm.

Sometimes we were given jobs on the boat, like swabbing the decks or polishing the brass.

When we got to New York, we only had our African clothes and sandals. But it was 10 degrees on the Brooklyn docks. We wrapped ourselves in blankets to keep warm. We saw the Statue of Liberty and the tall buildings and knew we had arrived! At the dock we saw our grandmother waiting for us, and, thank goodness, she had brought some warm clothes.

Blue Schoolhouse

It looks like we'll soon be back to regular school—probably not a "little red schoolhouse", but a big city school. Our "big blue schoolhouse" is over for now. What have we learned? Who knows. But this is something I'll always remember—spending time on the water, looking out at nothing but water, or looking up at nothing but stars.

THE END

Afterword

MATTHEW HERRON graduated from Stanford University in 1983 with an M.S. in Product Design, and since then has worked as a product design engineer for several major companies. He has been married for 25 years and has two sons and a daughter. From flying radio-controlled airplanes and gliders, he has graduated to owning his own sailplane. He loves soaring and flies with his father in cross-country competitions.

Top photo: Matthew and his dad getting ready to fly a sailplane in 2005.